KV-576-711

Batteries
and Bulbs

About Starters Science books

STARTERS SCIENCE books are designed to encourage scientific awareness in young children. The series aims to focus the instinctive curiosity of children and to encourage exploration and experiment. It also aims to develop language, encourage discussion and suggest situations where children can examine similarities and differences.

The text of each book is simple enough for children to read for themselves, and the vocabulary has been controlled to ensure that about 90 per cent of the words used will be familiar to them. Each book also contains a picture index and a page of notes for parents and teachers.

Written and planned by Albert James
Illustrator: Merle Lech

A MACDONALD BOOK

© Macdonald & Co (Publishers) Ltd 1973

First published in
Great Britain in 1973

Reprinted 1974, 1983 and 1986

All rights reserved

Printed and bound in Great Britain by
Hazell, Watson & Viney Ltd
Aylesbury, Buckinghamshire

Published by Macdonald & Co (Publishers) Ltd
Greater London House
Hampstead Road
London NW1 7QX

Members of BPCC plc

British Library Cataloguing in Publication Data
James, Albert
Batteries and bulbs. — (Starters science)
    1. Readers — 1950 —
    I. Title II. Series
    428.6   PE1119

ISBN 0-356-04447-5
ISBN 0-356-09283-6 Pbk

STARTERS
SCIENCE

Batteries
and Bulbs

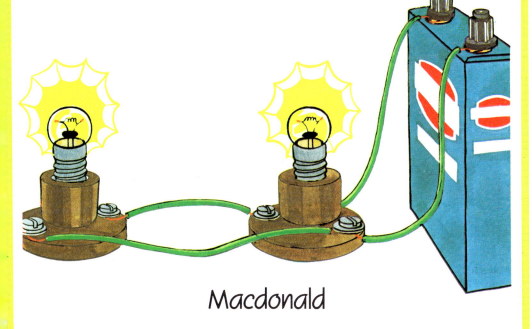

Macdonald

This man sells batteries and bulbs.

2

How many kinds of batteries can you see?
How many kinds of bulbs?

3

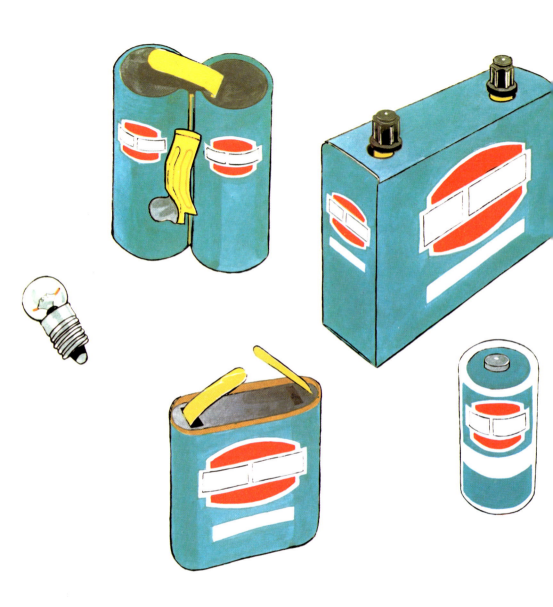

You will need these
to make the things in the book.

4

WARNING

NEVER experiment with mains electricity.
It is dangerous.
You are safe with the batteries in this book.

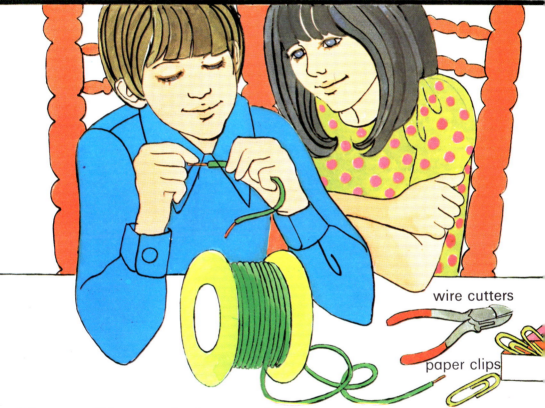

wire cutters

paper clips

You will need these things too.
The wire is made of copper.
It has a plastic cover.
Cut some plastic away from the ends.

If you join the wires up like this,
you can light the bulb.
Which part of the bulb
does the wire touch?

6

Use bulb holders like this.
Screw the wire on firmly.

Electricity goes through some things
but not others.
Is the bulb lit up?
Does electricity go through the pencil?

8

What things can electricity go through?
Test all kinds of things.

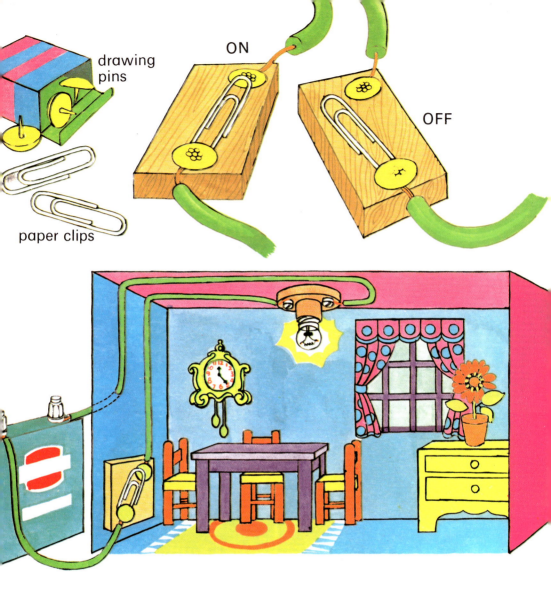

drawing pins

ON

OFF

paper clips

A switch is easy to make.
It puts the light on and off.
You could light up a model room.

10

transparent
plastic cup

sand

washing-up
liquid bottle

You can make a model lighthouse.
The light will flash
when you move the switch.

11

One battery can light two bulbs.
Which way works best?

12

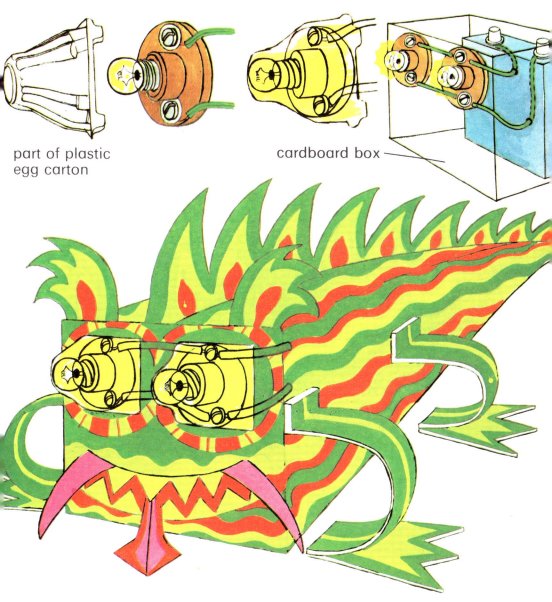

part of plastic
egg carton

cardboard box

This monster has eyes that flash
in the dark.
Can you make a monster?

13

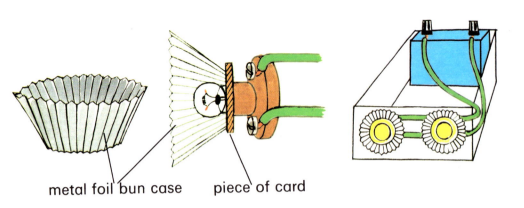

metal foil bun case   piece of card

You could make headlamps for a toy car.
What other things can you light?

14

rubber bands

ceiling tile

metal foil

paper clip

Can one battery light three bulbs?
Try some different ways.

cardboard scenery

metal foil reflector

bulbs behind foil

switch

Here is a little stage.
You can light your own theatre.
Put on a show for your friends.

16

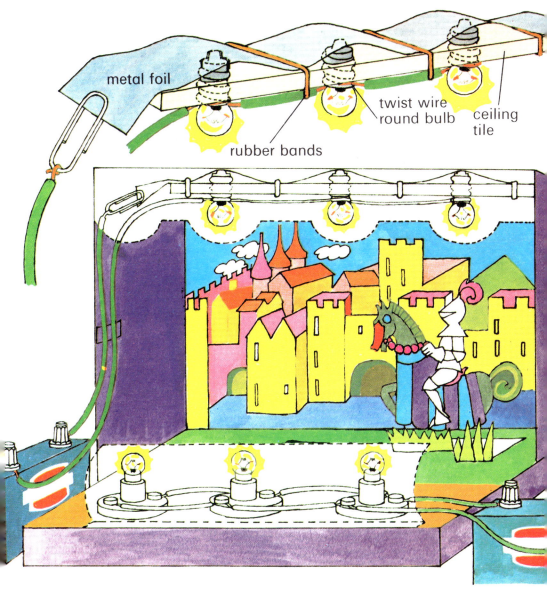

metal foil

twist wire
round bulb

ceiling
tile

rubber bands

Try using two batteries and six bulbs.
You could cover the bulbs
with thin coloured paper.

17

The car is waiting at the traffic lights.

18

red see-through paper

yellow see-through paper

green see-through paper

Make some model traffic lights.
How do you make the lights change?

19

We use many kinds of torches and lamps.
What kinds can you see in the picture?

20

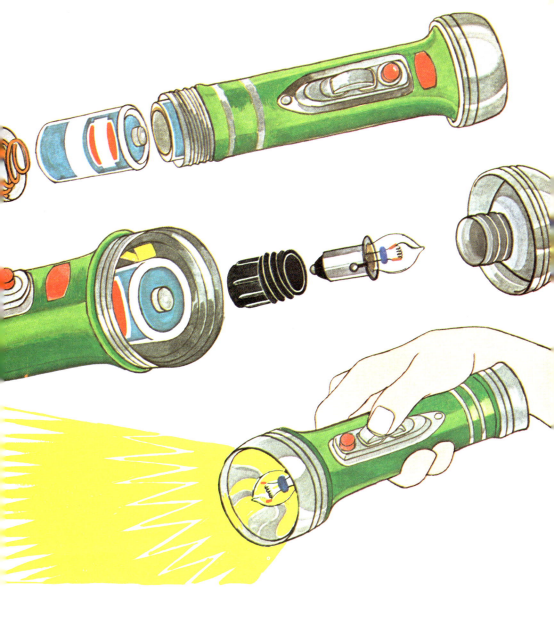

Do you know how to change a battery?
Can you put a new bulb into a torch?

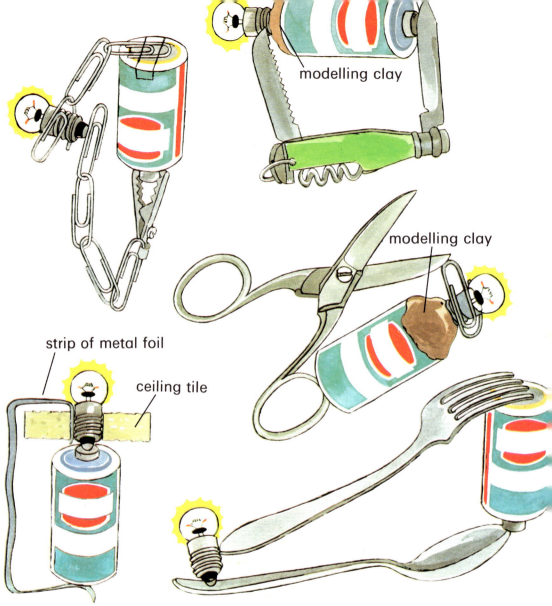

modelling clay

modelling clay

strip of metal foil

ceiling tile

Many torches use a battery like this one.
Can you use different things
to connect the bulb?

Try two batteries together.
What happens?

Try three batteries together.
Try all the ways you can think of.
Which works the best?

This is how a battery looks inside.
See how the parts are joined together.

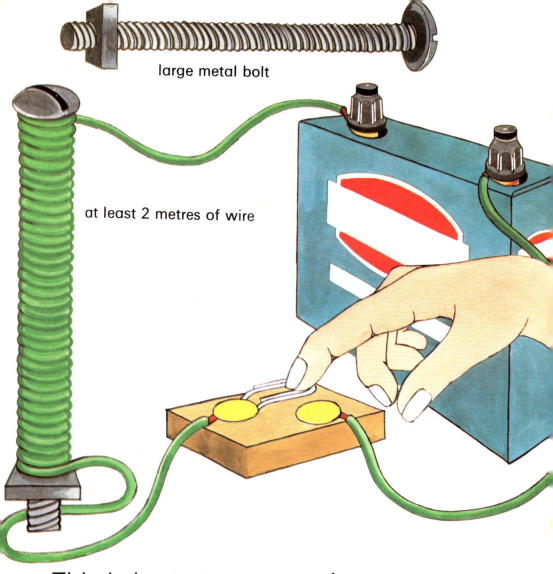

large metal bolt

at least 2 metres of wire

This is how you can make
an electro-magnet.
It uses a lot of electricity.
The battery will run down quickly.

26

What things will the magnet pick up?
What things won't it pick up?
Make two separate piles.

Index

Notes for Parents and Teachers

Starters Science books are designed for children to read and study on their own, but children would also benefit by sharing these topics with a parent or teacher. These brief notes explain the scientific ideas contained in the book, and help the interested adult to expand the themes.

2–5   These pages help to familiarise children with the different types of batteries and bulbs in common use; as well as to prepare them for the projects in the book.

6–10   The suggested projects will enable children to experiment with making connections between a battery and bulb, and introduce them to the idea of making a circuit. They are encouraged to discover conductors and insulators by means of simple experiments; and the construction of a switch may help to clarify the idea of a circuit; when the switch is off, the circuit is visibly broken.

12–19 During the course of a variety of projects, as well as by play and making toys, children are asked to explore series and parallel circuits.

20–22 These illustrate the different types of lamps and torches, and their various uses. Children are shown how to assemble a torch in the correct order, and encouraged to experiment further in conductivity.

23–25 Children are asked to observe the effects of connecting two or three batteries in different ways.

26–27 They are encouraged to discover magnetic and non-magnetic materials by experiments, and to make and learn about electromagnets.